SNAP BACKS

by
MARISSA MICHAELS

SCHOLASTIC INC.
New York   Toronto   London   Auckland   Sydney

ISBN 0-590-02583-X

12 11 10 9 8 7 6 5 4 3 2 1   7 8 9/9 0 1 2/0
Printed in U.S.A.   01

First Scholastic printing, March 1997

You're on your way to homeroom. Walking straight toward you is the school bully. As he passes you, he growls, "What are you looking at?"

You're tempted to say, "Nothing," but you know that will get you into big trouble. If only, just once, you could think of the perfect thing to say. Something that would make his face turn red with embarrassment. But what could you say?

Think, think. Think faster. Wait, it's coming! Just one more minute....

Too late. He's already down the hall, out the door, and having a hamburger at the diner.

Stop thinking and start reading SNAPBACKS. Now you'll have the perfect put-down for any occasion.

So come on, snap to it! It's your turn to Snap Back!

SNAP BACKS

You remind me of the ocean.
You never dry up.

I wish you were on TV so I could
turn you off.

You're out of this world.
I hope you stay there.

When I look at you, time stands
still.
Your face can stop a clock.

Want to see something funny?
Look in the mirror.

Please don't give me a piece of your mind — you can't spare it.

You have the face of a saint — a St. Bernard.

You should try to get ahead.
You certainly could use one.

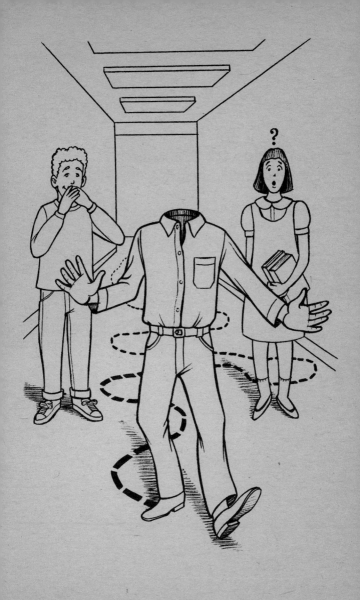

You couldn't carry a tune even if it were in a backpack.

FAMILY FEUD

When my brother was born they fired twenty-one guns. Unfortunately, they all missed.

My sister never has anything to say, but that doesn't stop her from saying it.

The only thing my sister exercises is her tongue.

My brother is so stupid he ate a whole jar of mustard because somebody told him he was full of baloney.

My sister is so stupid. Her boyfriend asked to see her home so she showed him a photograph of it.

My brother is so ugly that when he goes to the zoo he has to buy two tickets — one to get in and another to get out.

Sometimes my parents would like to change their name to protect the innocent.

Mom: At your age I could name all of the Presidents in the proper order.

Tom: Sure — but there were only four or five of them then.

My brother is so stupid he's written TGIF on his shoes — Toes Go In First!

Little sis: I'm pretending to be a princess.

Big sis: I'm pretending I don't know you.

Sister: Have you forgotten that you owe me five dollars?

Brother: No. Not yet. Give me time and I will.

Dad: I slept like a log last night.

Lad: You certainly did. I heard you sawing it.

Mom: Look here. I was cooking
  meals long before you were born.
Son: Okay, but why serve them now?

My mother treats me like a goddess.
She gives me burnt offerings at
every meal.

Dad: Your room is such a mess. You're a pig. Do you know what a pig is?

Kid: Sure. A pig is a hog's little boy.

FRIENDLY FIRE

Girl: Do you know her to speak to?
Friend: No. Only to talk about.

Sal: I'm not myself tonight.
Cal: Then we ought to have a good
time.

Jerry: Do you know how I keep my head above water?

Terry: Sure. Wood floats.

Ron: When you die, you ought to leave your head to science.

Don: Why?

Ron: They're still trying to find the perfect vacuum.

Sally: Did you notice how my voice filled the theater last night?

Hallie: Yes. I even noticed people leaving to make room for it.

Phil: I passed your house today.
Will: Thanks. I appreciate it.

Mary: I'll always have a soft spot in my heart for you.

John: Then let's get married.

Mary: I said a soft spot in my heart, not in my head.

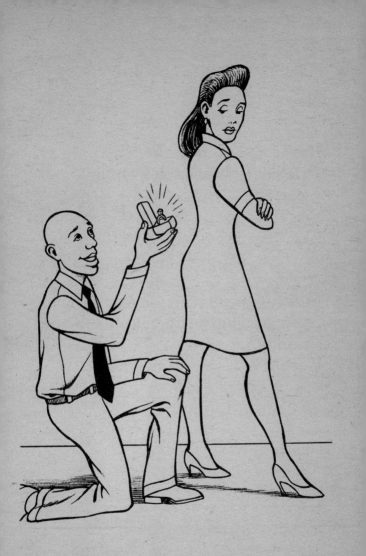

Boy: I can imitate any bird.
Friend: How about a homing
pigeon?

Mary: I spend hours in front of the
mirror admiring my beauty. Is that
vanity?
Kate: No, it's your imagination.

Matt: I wish I had been born in the Dark Ages.

Pat: So do I. You look terrible in the light.

Girl: I hope I haven't kept you up too late.

Friend: Not at all. I would be getting up soon anyway.

Joy: Whenever I'm down in the dumps, I get a new dress.

Roy: From the looks of the one you're wearing, that must be where you got it.

Sue: A little bird told me that you were going to buy me a ring.
Lou: It must have been a cuckoo.

Ann: I just got an idea.
Lee: Beginner's luck.

Bob: I'd love to see you in something
flowing.
Carol: A long gown?
Bob: The river.

Your problem is that you always say what you think...without thinking.

Fred: My mind is going.
Ed: It won't be a long trip.

Bill: Will you join me?
Michelle: Why? Are you coming apart?

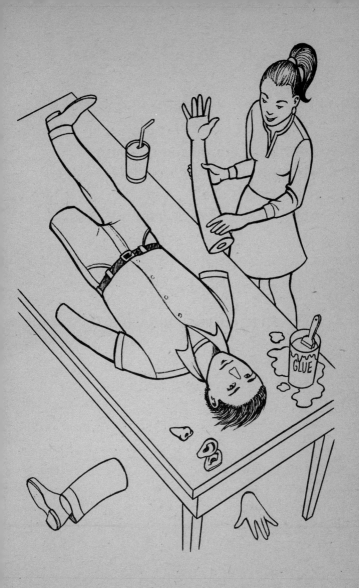

Boy: You remind me of a shirt button.

Girl: How's that?

Boy: You're always popping off.

Bob: Did you miss me when I was gone?

Rob: Were you gone?

Pat: Don't you think I sing with feeling?

Nat: No — if you had any feeling you wouldn't sing.

Harry: That's a nice suit you're wearing.

Larry: Do you like it?

Harry: Yes. Who went for the fitting?

CLASS-LESS COMEBACKS

Teacher: I wish you'd pay a little attention.

Greg: I'm paying as little attention as possible.

Student: I don't think that I deserved a zero on this paper.

Teacher: Neither do I, but it's the lowest grade I can give.

Sal: Teacher, do you think someone should be punished for something they didn't do?

Teacher: Of course not.

Sal: In that case — I didn't do my homework.

Teacher to student: I always knew you had a photographic mind. Too bad it was never developed.

Teacher: Are you studying to be an astronaut?

Student: Why?

Teacher: You're certainly taking up space.

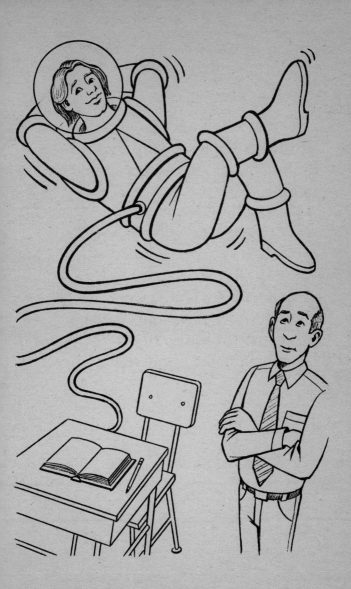

Student: My teacher is such a bore, even my foot falls asleep when she's talking.

Teacher: Why is it you can never answer any of my questions?
Student: If I could, there wouldn't be much point in my coming here.

Teacher: You should have been in school at nine o'clock.
Amy: Why — did I miss something?

Teacher: Why are you always late for school?
Dawn: Because you're always ringing the bell before I get here.

Teacher: What's your excuse for being late this time?

Student: There was a notice on the bus that said dogs must be carried and my brother refused to jump into my arms.

NOTICE:

ALL DOGS
MUST BE
CARRIED

Student: I was the teacher's pet. He couldn't afford a dog.

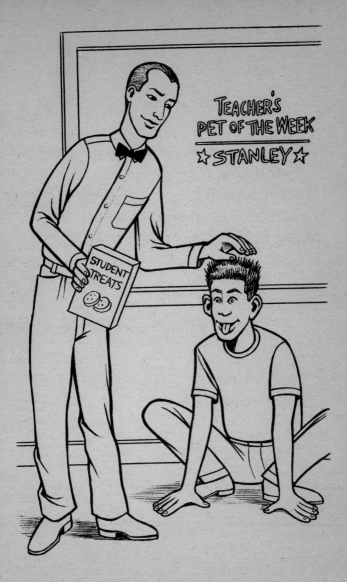

Teacher: Why weren't you at school yesterday?

Matt: I was sick.

Teacher: Sick of what?

Matt: Sick of school.

Teacher: Would you like to ask me a question?

Student: When are you going?

Teacher: I hope I didn't see you looking at Alex's paper.
Student: I hope so, too.

Teacher: I've got to give you credit, Bobby. You're always trying — very trying.

Ted: My mother doesn't like going to parent-teacher conferences.

Alice: Why not?

Ted: She says the teacher makes everything sound so simple — including me.

Word to the wise: Making faces at your girlfriend in class may be very romantic, but she may not want to grow up and marry an idiot.

RIGHT BACK AT YA!

The day you were born you cried
like a baby.
So did the rest of your family.

You're just like a fence.
You run around a lot but you never
get anywhere.

You must get up very early in the
morning.
How else could you do so many
stupid things in one day?

You have what it takes.
I only wish you'd take it
someplace else.

I'd like to help you out.
Which way did you come in?

You could talk your head off and never miss it.

You're a sight for sore eyes — a real eyesore.

You're good looking in a way.
Away off.

If you had to eat your words, you'd get an upset stomach.

One of us is crazy.
But don't worry — I'll keep your
secret.

You seem to have so much get up
and go.
So why don't you?

You remind me of a jigsaw puzzle —
so many of the pieces are missing.

Why don't you...

. . . act like a magician and disappear?

. . . make like a knife and cut out?

. . . make like a tree and leave?

. . . make like a drum and beat it?

. . . make like a tissue and blow?

. . . make like a nose and run?

. . . make like a pack of cards and shuffle off?

CLASS
7B

. . . hop on your broom and fly away?

. . . make like a banana and split?

. . . make like a scale and go weigh?

. . . make like a rubber band and snap out of here?

. . . make like a dancer and go-go?

. . . make like a ball and roll away?

RIGHT BACK AT YA — AGAIN!

I don't want to have a battle of wits
with you.
I never attack anyone who's
unarmed.

You have one of those mighty
minds — mighty empty.

I'm really happy to see you're back —
especially after seeing your face.

You remind me of a film star —
Lassie.

You're so stupid you think cows wear bells because their horns don't work.

You shouldn't let your mind wander.
It might not come back.

You remind me of a goat — always butting in.

You have such a big mouth you could eat a banana sideways.

Your ideas are like diamonds —
very rare.

PARTING SHOTS

You're the kind you have to look at twice — the first time you just don't believe it.

Tim: You dance beautifully.
Jill: I wish I could say the same for you.
Tim: You could if you were as good a liar as I am.

My boyfriend is so weak, when he tries to whip cream, the cream wins.

Ike: You'd better keep your eyes open today.
Mike: Why?
Ike: If you don't, you'll keep banging into things.

You sing like a bird and have a brain
to match.

If I've said anything to offend you,
please let me know.
I might want to say it again.